an extract from
iain crichton smith's
murdo
the life and works
with an enthusiast's view
by douglas gifford

Scottish **Book** Trust

an extract from
iain crichton smith's
murdo
the life and works
with an enthusiast's view
by douglas gifford

2003

Published by
Scottish Book Trust
Scottish Book Centre
137 Dundee Street
Edinburgh EH11 1BG

Tel: 0131 229 3663

**From April 2003 Scottish Book Trust will be moving its offices
to Sandeman House, 55 High Street, Edinburgh EH1 1SR.**

ISBN: 1 901077 01 2
Copyright © Scottish Book Trust, 2003

Published with the support of the Scottish Arts Council National
Lottery Fund and The Hugh Fraser Foundation.

Murdo: The Life and Works is published by Birlinn Ltd
ISBN 1 84158 058 9

Extract copyright © Iain Crichton Smith, 1981

Series design by Caleb Rutherford   eidetic
Printed in the UK by Cox & Wyman, Reading, Berkshire

contents

read **around books**

There is no shortage of fiction on the shelves of our bookshops – quite the opposite – but finding one that shouts out 'this is what you are looking for' is getting harder and harder as the number of books published goes up with each passing year. Too often we open a new book with expectation and enthusiasm only to discover disappointment and to struggle to get beyond page thirty. When we do find a book we really enjoy the urge is there to tell friends, colleagues and family to read it too in the hope that they will share our delight.

Read Around Books goes one step further and puts that enthusiasm down in black and white in the hope that many more readers will discover the joys of reading the very finest fiction that has emerged from Scotland over the last one hundred years. **This is a chance to sample before you borrow or buy**. Others have found these books before you, the writing held them spellbound and even when finished, these books would not let their readers go.

Each of the first twelve of these highly collectable little guide books promotes a work of fiction by a writer who lives in Scotland, was born in Scotland or who has been influenced by Scotland (our definition of Scottish is generous). Together they offer a marvellous introduction to the very best of Scottish writing from the twentieth and the first few years of the twenty-first centuries.

In each you will find a substantial extract, the enthusiast's view of the book, starting points for discussion for readers' groups, a short biographical piece about the author, and suggestions for similar reads which act as a further gateway to fine fiction.

Jan Rutherford
Series editor, 2003

the enthusiast

Douglas Gifford

Douglas Gifford is Professor of Scottish literature at the University of Glasgow. He is also a well known and respected literary critic and a member of the judging panel for the annual Saltire Literary Awards. He has recently finished co-editing *Scottish Literature* (Edinburgh University Press, 2002), a companion to Scottish literature from the medieval period to the close of the twentieth century.

the enthusiast's **view**

Murdo: The Life and Works
by Iain Crichton Smith

There is no-one quite like Murdo and nothing quite like his disturbing adventures and ruminations anywhere else in Scottish and British literature. His nearest Scottish cousin is probably the mad Victorian Scottish poet William McGonagall, though Murdo has genius of a demented sort which his Dundee kinsman has not. His unique blend of comedy and tragedy, sense and lunacy, controlled satire and angry despair links him with some famous Europeans, like Don Quixote and the Good Soldier Schweik. His concerns and agonies, however, are tied tightly to those of his creator (and alter ego) Iain Crichton Smith, and Smith's tormented relationship with his Lewis background and family and their introspective community, culture and stern Free Church religion on one hand, and what Smith felt as the increasing senselessness of Western and world affairs and culture on the other.

Murdo's creator Iain Crichton Smith (1928-1998) is one of Scotland's greatest poets and novelists. Born in Glasgow in 1928, he was brought up and educated in staunchly Presbyterian Lewis, with a devout Free Church mother; thence to the University of Aberdeen, National Service, and then teaching in Clydebank and Oban till 1977; thereafter continuing to live near Oban as a full-time writer. His Lewis and Gaelic experience left him with a deep distrust of the church (he admitted to wanting to punch Free Church ministers on the nose), and a later guilt regarding his neglect of his Gaelic cultural roots. To this must be added his complex feelings of love and disagreement with his strong-willed mother, who lived in Lewis with her sons in poverty after the death of her husband. Smith works her endlessly into his poems and stories, recognising both her stubborn intolerance and her self-denial; she was to work as a fishgutter while Iain studied English and Classics at university. She is the model for his sympathetic portrayal in his first novel, *Consider the Lilies* (1968), of the plight of Widow Scott, a stern, lonely old woman under threat of eviction from her home in the time of the Highland Clearances.

This kind of disguising frequently occurs in Smith's fiction. Readers intrigued by the Murdo stories will be equally, if differently, intrigued by the compelling, distressing and yet sometimes hilariously zany account of mental breakdown close to Smith's own experience, *In The Middle of the Wood* (1987). Less shockingly, many of his own dilemmas and guilts were faced in the many novels which followed, together with his fundamental doubts concerning the relevance of great art and high culture to the lives of ordinary people – and indeed his doubts that the poet (or even teacher) of today had any place in a hard materialistic world. These doubts contributed to his own nervous breakdowns, and are astonishingly and therapeutically translated into art in his Murdo stories – where the reader's suspicions that Murdo speaks for many of Smith's concerns are finally borne out in the last section of the book, the until now unpublished 'Life of Murdo'. In a brief preface to the 'Life', Smith admits that 'many people will be surprised that in my autobiography the main character should be Murdo. Murdo, however, is my alter ego as revealed in *Thoughts of Murdo* published some years ago. Using 'Murdo' rather than 'I' allowed me the distance that I needed to be objective about myself and to make comedy of painful experiences'. It is poignant to realise that this admission came not long before Smith's death in 1998; and striking to think that the bizarre humour of these apparently surreal stories held a deeply serious purpose and meaning. They allowed a kind of redemption from breakdown for Smith, who found, as did Walpole, that life is a tragedy to those who feel, and a comedy to those who think (however strangely!).

So Smith created Murdo, the ex-bank clerk turned would-be writer, economically impoverished and embarrassingly unpredictable in word and deed, yet unflinchingly supported by Janet against the contempt of relatives as he fulminates (with what seems to be at first like plain lunacy) against what he perceives as a world filled with injustice and stupidity, from the crass commercialism of TV and the unfairness of Arts Councils to the anachronisms of the Mod and the untimeliness of MacBrayne's boats. The first Murdo story (simply called 'Murdo') appeared in 1981, well before the 1993 volume *Thoughts of Murdo*, the sixty-seven or so random musings which make up the middle section of this book; with the 'Life' appended here now as Smith's final offering and admission. And it is worth recognising the very different tone and intention of that first long story from subsequent offerings. Underlying all its grotesque humour (Murdo's wearing of the red nose while unsettling his neighbours with his weather banalities and his warnings that Calvin is alive and living in a nearby croft, his importuning of frightened librarians for the locally written version of *War and Peace* or the Karamazov story of three brothers and a croft) lies a profound agony. It concerns the ageing and death of Murdo's father, whose face 'glared gauntly' at Murdo with Murdo's own face 'set as stone'. The story concludes with 'that grey question' for Janet and Murdo – which is the question as to life's meaning and end. The white mountain which Murdo gazes at throughout is not just a real mountain like Ben Cruachan, but a symbol of an uncaring universe.

If there was a silent scream throughout this first story, the 'Thoughts' which followed in the following decade showed that Smith had discovered a persona who could express and control his pain and anger through surreal humour. Smith's anger at being forbidden Gaelic at school is channelled into Murdo's deceptively childish opening story which somehow underscores the damage done to the child's mind; Murdo's abandoning the bank (which likes to say yes) echoes Smith's rejection of schoolteaching. Smith's legendary dislike of television's intrusion into real life becomes Murdo's warning to the prime minister that most people now think that life is a TV documentary. Sometimes Murdo simply seems to express Smith's love of the surreal for its own sake – as in Murdo's idea of sending his daughter to the moon, or his suggestion that the Mod should take place in Paris since there are so many Gaels left there after a football international (and since the Gaelic *eaglais* for church is so like the French *église*). More tellingly, his Portree detective stories featuring Sam Spaid, the Free Church private investigator, slyly expose the petty narrrow-mindedness and the utter un-romance which Smith all too often finds in his Gaelic communities. And most tellingly of all, a dark satirical commentary runs through the majority, as in the not-so-ludicrous idea that Calvin is alive and well (so Murdo reports him to the police); or that Portree (and Gaeldom) lacks educated people, because they have all gone to work for the BBC; and in the marvellous parodies, somehow managing to maintain a weird and unsettling poetry of their own, of Highland prophecies – 'When the access card is lost there will be sorrow in the glen'; 'The end of the world is near when the MacBrayne's ship shall be on time'; 'The man who sings through the nose will signify the downfall of the Mod'; 'The MacLeods of Skye will submit to the papers from the far country'. A latter-day Brahan Seer, Smith manages simultaneously to mock the cloudy generalities of so-called second sight while teasing the reader with hints of all-too-sane social criticism.

This volume describes a sensitive man's progress from tragedy, through comedy, to a moving acceptance. Readers who enjoy it – and these stories have a cult following! – may wish to follow Smith's journey in poetry and prose at a slower and more reflective pace. Suggested starting points are listed in the further reading section of this small book.

The extract

Murdo:

The Life and Works

Murdo

One day Murdo said to his wife, 'Shall we climb that white mountain?'

'No,' she said with astonishment. 'It's too cold.'

Murdo looked around him. The chairs were shining in the light like precious stones. The curtains were shimmering with light as if they were water. The table was standing on its four precious legs. His wife in her blue dress was also precious and precious also was the hum of the pan on the cooker. 'I remember,' he told his wife, 'when I was young I used to listen every Sunday to the sound of the pot boiling on the fire. We had herring all during the week.'

'We too,' said his wife, 'but we had meat on Sunday.' She was thinking that Murdo wasn't looking too well and this frightened her. But she didn't say anything to him.

'Herring,' said Murdo, 'what would we do without it? The salt herring, the roasted herring. The herring that swims through the sea among the other more royal fish. So calm. So sure of itself.'

'One day my father killed a rabbit with his gun,' said his wife.

'I'm sure,' said Murdo.

'I'm telling the truth,' Janet insisted.

'I'm not denying it,' said Murdo as he watched the shimmering curtains. And the table shone in front of him, solid and precious and fixed, and the sun glittered all over the room.

O my happiness, he said to himself. O my happiness. How happy the world is without me. How the world doesn't need me. If only I could remember that. The table is so calm and fixed, without soul, single and without turmoil, the chairs compose a company of their own.

'Come on, let's dance,' he said to Janet.

'What, now?' she said.

'Yes,' said Murdo, 'now. Let's dance now.'

'All right then,' said Janet.

And they began to dance among the chairs, and the pan shone red in a corner of its own.

And Murdo recalled how they had used to dance in their youth on the autumn nights with the moon above them and his heart so full that it was like a bucket full of water, almost spilling over.

At last Janet sat down, as she was breathless.

And Murdo sat on a chair beside her.

'Well, well,' said he, 'we must do that oftener.'

'Oh the pan,' said his wife and she ran over to the cooker where the pan was boiling over.

The pan, said Murdo to himself, the old scarred pan. It also is dancing.

On its own fire.

Everything is dancing, said Murdo, if we only knew it. The whole world is dancing. The lion is dancing and the lamb is dancing. Good is dancing with Evil in an eternal reel in an invisible light. And he thought of them for a moment, Good and Evil, with their arms around each other on a fine autumn evening with the dew falling steadily and invisibly on the grass.

Thoughts of Murdo

Murdo & The Spaceship

When I arrived at Murdo's house I found him working on a big machine while another man was sitting on a chair with a melodeon. Murdo's daughter, Mary, was asking him how the spaceship was coming . . .

Murdo said, 'I need paraffin. Morag doesn't have any in the shop. She's got everything else, spades, rinso, mince, bread, margarine, guided missiles, but no paraffin.' His thick glasses glittered contemptuously.

'Well, I'm sure it won't be long till you get your paraffin,' said Mary. 'Do you need anything else?'

'I need four-inch nails,' said her father, 'but Kenneth here got them for me in New York. He was playing at a

Gaelic festival there, weren't you, Kenneth?'

'Indeed I was,' said Kenneth, who was bald and had a very thin neck.

'Kenneth here is a sex symbol,' said Murdo. 'He was playing at this festival and he went into a shop in 42nd Street. The man who owned it was from Skye. It took him three years to reach America on MacBrayne's and then he was attacked by some Red Indians from Harris. Isn't that right, Kenneth?'

'That's right,' said Kenneth.

'And what are you going to do with the spaceship, father?' said Mary.

'It's not a spaceship. It's a rocket,' said Murdo. 'I thought at first of directing it against Moscow but then I thought Moscow hasn't done anything to me so I'll attack MacBrayne's with it instead.'

'It's high time you launched the rocket, father,' said Mary. 'I can't reach the wardrobe because of it.'

'The wardrobe,' said Murdo.

'Yes, where I keep the clothes.'

'Oh, the wardrobe. I can't understand how you can think of trivialities like that in this technological age,' said Murdo. 'Surely you know that I have spent seven years on this project. Seven years when I could have been doing something else.'

'Like what?' said Mary.

'Well, building an anti-ballistic shield,' said Murdo.

'When do you intend to launch the rocket?' said Mary.

At that point a little woman dressed in black and carrying a Bible bound with elastic came in.

'Oh, here's Anna,' said Murdo. 'Were you in church, Anna?'

'Yes, indeed,' said Anna. 'The text was from Exodus. A good minister. Strong voice. Fine hairstyle.'

'What did you say?' said Murdo.

'Oh, I'm in a rage,' Anna said, 'Jessie was wearing the same kind of hat as me.'

After a while, Murdo said in a serious voice, 'Anna.'

'Yes,' said Anna.

'Would you like to go to the moon, Anna?'

'To the moon?' said Anna, in a surprised voice.

'Surely, father, you're not sending Anna to the moon,' said Mary. 'You promised me I could go to the moon. I bought a new frock for it.'

'You keep quiet, Mary,' said Murdo angrily.

He turned to Anna. 'The thing is, Anna, do you think you'd be able to handle the media? The media is very important.'

'Media? What's that?' said Anna.

'The newspapers, the BBC, the television,' said Murdo.

'Oh, I can speak to them right enough,' said Anna. 'What do I have to say?'

'Father,' said Mary.

'You keep quiet,' said Murdo. 'I want a religious woman to land on the moon. A woman who can sing a psalm. Can you do that, Anna?'

'Oh, I can sing a psalm right enough,' said Anna. 'But you want me to do it on the moon?'

'Think of it, Anna,' said Murdo. 'You'll be standing on the moon, in your black mini-skirt with your fish-net stockings. Real fish-net. Of course, we'll take the corks out of it first. You will be a sex symbol for the whole world.'

'I would like that,' said Anna.

'And now for the big day,' said Murdo, taking out his diary. 'It can't be Thursday. That's early closing day. Or Sunday. You can't go to the moon on a Sunday, Anna.'

'No, I couldn't do that,' said Anna.

'Tuesday would be all right,' said Murdo. 'Are you free on Tuesday?'

'Tuesday,' said Anna. 'Oh, I don't know about Tuesday. That's my Hate the Catholics night.'

'Well, what about Wednesday then?' said Murdo. 'You don't go to the bingo on a Wednesday, do you?'

'No, I don't go to the bingo,' said Anna. 'Wednesday would be all right.'

'I'll put that in my diary then,' said Murdo. 'You're not frightened are you.'

'Not at all,' said Anna.

'And you're not afraid of communicating with the media? You must be sharp and quick, Anna. What will you say to them when they ask you why you joined the mission to the moon?'

'I'll say, this is a big step for mankind but especially for Gravir.'

'Oh, there is one other thing,' said Murdo. 'Is there anything suspicious or immoral in your background, Anna? You can expect a lot of probing. The media is ruthless.'

'Immoral?' said Anna.

'Yes, like incest, murder, theft, speaking to Catholics. Anything like that?'

'No, no,' said Anna, 'nothing at all like that.'

'That's good, Anna. And now we'll sing Amazing Grace. What about Amazing Grace, Kenneth? Give us Amazing Grace.'

Kenneth sang Amazing Grace, but not well. 'It's all right,' said Murdo. 'Kenneth here is more used to Country and Western. What's wrong, Anna?'

'I've just remembered. I can't go on Wednesday.'

'Why not?' said Murdo.

'It's the day I collect my pension,' said Anna.

Murdo gnashed his teeth with frustration and chased her out.

'That means Mary here will have to go after all,' he said.

Murdo's Random Jottings

A foot in both cramps.

Flogging a head nurse.

A snake in the grass keeps one on one's toes.

An apple a day keeps the orange away.

He left under a shroud.

No man is an island but Harris is.

Duty is only skin keep.

A stitch in nine saves time.
Thyme is of the essence.
A putter wouldn't melt in his mouth.
Sneaking about is the better part of valour.
Casting your Fred upon the waters.
It's all ill wind that does not recover.
Turning the other sheikh.
The tigers of luxury succumb to the warthogs of
    righteousness.
The herring volk – people of Peterhead.
My art's in the Highlands – Van Och.
A woman's place is in a home.
All that glitters is not lead.
There's no fire without smoke.
Incidents will happen.
Here be dragoons.
People in grass skirts shouldn't throw cinders.
If you can't stand the heat get out of the furnace.
The first shall be last and the last shall be fifth.
Sand Ahoy!
Never say Dai.
Helping a lame writer over his style.
Going to work on a leg.

Life of Murdo

At the age of seventy, Murdo would look back on his life in between visiting the toilet and scraping dry skin from behind his ears. He was brought up in a small village of churchgoers, football players and men with long beards. He was totally useless at everything he touched. He could not use a scythe, he could not cut peats, he could not clean the chimney. He would stand for hours staring at a cow or a sunset.

People would say about Murdo, he is so stupid he must be very clever. Actually nothing much went on in Murdo's head. He was very poor, and would be sent by his mother to ask people for money. He thought happiness was a scone with crowdie or the back of a loaf with marmalade. He could not afford mutton or beef. Sometimes as he lay in his bed in the small house of one bedroom and mean furniture he would dream of chocolates, but never of theology. He would have given away the whole Bible for a slice of melon.

Oh those dreaming days between moor and sea. Murdo never went on a boat but loved looking for hours into soupy pools where crabs moved sideways. He loved mussels and whelks and foamy seas on stormy days. He drew pictures of drifters, and motor boats.

And he read a great deal: that was his solace. The books he read were *Black Masks* imported from America and borrowed from one particular friend. The criminals wore masks and the detective was as much hunted by the police as by the criminals. Murdo never related these stories to his mother as he thought there were worse in the Bible. He could not have survived if he had not read. In woodwork, however, the teachers thought he had problems with his coordination: thus, a simple table he had made might look like a bed post and vice versa. He also had great difficulty in tying his laces. Under his breath he would often mutter the words 'Horse manure' which he had picked up from his *Black Mask* books.

There was no toilet in the house and no hot water. The roof was made of felt. There was a bed in the kitchen and one in the bedroom. He loved Rupert in the *Daily Express*. He used to go to the well for water and to the moor for his toilet. While squatting there benignly he would hum Gaelic tunes but he would not yet think of the Clearances of which he had not heard at that time. Indeed he had not heard much of the history of the island and had not visited many parts of it, as there were no cars, and he would immediately have got lost anyway. He had no sense of direction and would often turn left to find himself at the edge of a dangerous cliff.

He knew more about Dickens and *Black Mask* than he knew about his village. He loved *Oliver Twist* for instance. He imagined London as a place where there were toilets and hot water and people didn't have to go to wells.

Sometimes as he walked across the linoleum in the

early morning he would have an impulse to sing. However, at school he was often bullied. He was nicknamed the Bird because he was up in the air all the time. Now and again the teachers would belt him for muttering 'Horse manure'. He loved certain words such as 'macabre' or 'marauder'. But essays such as 'A Day in the Life of a Penny' would not allow him to use them. One of the teachers was grey and spectral and loved cemeteries. She gave them sweets but nevertheless they tormented her. At the end of the day, pupils from different villages would fire stones at each other. Thus what later he saw on TV about Israel and the Palestinians seemed quite familiar to him. People were always coming up and offering to fight him. He was always being knocked down and the woollen suits his mother made for him mocked. In summer like the others he went barefoot. In any case he could hardly afford shoes.

One time he wrote a piece about Neville Chamberlain who travelled all over Europe with an umbrella as a protection against Nazism. He read this to his family who were not impressed. His brother tore up the ending of a story about Wild Bill Hickock and ever afterwards he hated him and even now between going on visits to the toilet he remembers that incident quite clearly.

Once, walking in a ditch, he was hit by a shinty stick with which a scholar was taking practice swings. A lump rose rapidly on his head.

He was often ill with bronchitis and thrust into bed by his mother who always wore black because she was a widow. 'Stay there,' she would say to him, 'or you will die of tuberculosis of which there is much about and of which your father who drank a lot of whisky died.' So Murdo spent weeks and weeks in bed, reading books about public schoolboys in England. He thought death was round the corner and that he would die young. But he never did, and now he is seventy and hale and hearty and receives his pension. Such is life, and the working of predestination.

Murdo however played a little football and loved to do so. Sometimes himself and another young villager would play with a fishing cork. Without his reading and his football he would not have become the drooling geriatric he is today. There was no TV in those days, only wirelesses as big as wardrobes. The wirelesses were run by batteries for there was no electricity in Murdo's house. The wireless would tell him how the English international football team beat the Scottish international football team by seven goals to nothing.

Murdo would collect cigarette cards, some with footballers on them, some with flowers. Around the house he would not tread on the daisies lest he should injure them. He recognised no other flowers and indeed there weren't many others. However he hated seagulls and would throw stones at them. As also at the telegraph wires. He was as cruel as everybody else to a fat woman with fat red legs who lived in a thatched house with ten cats and wasn't all there. He only learnt pity from his own later suffering.

This story Murdo is telling now to pass the time between going to the toilet and scraping dry skin from his head. Old age, he will have you know, is not romantic, but itchy and wet. His bodily functions are all failing. He uses all sorts of powders, creams, air fresheners, eye drops, scalp cleansers, and so on. All he thinks about is food but he does not drink so much now, as it makes him depressed.

He looks out of the window a lot and thinks up nicknames for people. He considers sending anonymous letters full of murderous intent to game hosts on television.

Nevertheless he is at times content and makes up new versions of old poems such as this by Milton:

When I consider what my wife has spent
in Marks and Spencers I have screamed and cried.

And so on.

Murdo rested for a moment in his narrative, absently plucking a scab from his scalp and scratching at his itchy eyes.

Murdo in his youth was surrounded by tuberculosis. Oh yes, the young as well as the old were dying of it. Their faces grew white, they spat and spat, they coughed their little dry coughs, they went to the sanatorium, and they died.

And Murdo in his youth was surrounded by war. His friends were drowned in foreign seas. He listened to the wireless and heard of their lost ships. He heard names like *Timoshenko* and *Voroshilov*, he ate whale meat and put saccharines in his tea. And his brother was in the Navy as an officer.

Murdo attended secondary school and learnt about

Pythagoras's theorem from the well-loved Caney who spat all over his geometry book and who had been engaged for twenty-five years to a lady from the Science Dept.

And one day he was strapped for not learning from the New Testament, the famous passage about charity and tinkling cymbals.

Oh Murdo was not well fed at all. At dinner intervals he would go to the Reading Room in the town and pore over magazines which showed fox-hunting people and shrivelled women sharing a joke. Ha ha think of poor Murdo wondering what sharing a joke meant. And there were leather covers on these magazines.

Was he clever? No, he was not. But he loved Mr Trail, his Latin teacher, who when the bell went would leave the staffroom, having already opened his Vergil, and who would walk along the corridor, the book open in front of him, feel for the handle of the door and say, 'Line 340, Catriona.' Mr Trail was a ball of fire and had hair like a fox.

And Murdo loved Dido and hated Aeneas.

And he loved Vergil.

The war raged on and he ate salt fish and there were no oranges.

And he fell in love with a girl with bluish black hair. One day he climbed over a wall, to bring her a piece of turnip. And he wept and cried, and that was a long time ago, and he met her many years afterwards and he could not believe that this was she. And maybe, thought Murdo, this is not she at all.

One time Murdo had gone to bed after studying his

theorems and Rob, his friend who was in the Navy and home on leave, came in to say goodbye. He came over to the bed and Murdo could not open his eyes. He never saw Rob again.

Murdo was as thin as a pencil. There was no flesh on him at all. He was continually aware of his own uselessness. And he was aware of the Atlantic and the deserts of North Africa and the snows of Russia. But he was not aware that there was any oddity in lack of toilets, electricity and running water. (No *en suite* for Murdo.)

Sometimes there would be storms and hens being driven on to the moors by the wind.

And another time he went to the house of a fat spinster woman and she and another fat spinster woman were talking in sexual terms. And Murdo picked up the women's magazine where in a story a woman stabbed a rival with a pair of scissors. This troubled him for a while, indeed gave him nightmares. The sound of the sea was in his ears every day. He read Keats and many other poets, and he kept a big notebook in which he wrote poems. But he never showed them to anyone.

The war raged on. And he read his *Black Mask* stories. He loved geometry more than anything except the crosswords in the *Listener*. And there was *Titbits*, and *Answers* also. His mother didn't like the villagers whose cows chewed her clothes on the line though the villagers were good to her. But she never had any money and she was a widow and she had come from another village. And she always talked about Glasgow where she had lived when young: and of Blochairn and Parliamentary

Rd. etc. That was before Murdo's father died, who had been a seaman. Ah, what a terrible life Murdo's mother led. She never had anything new, she was dependent on others, she had a widow's small pension, and she had to count every halfpenny.

She grasped Murdo with a grip of death lest he should get TB.

And Murdo would sit in the attic reading D.H. Lawrence and *No Orchids for Miss Blandish*, for this is how he learned about sex.

The larks sang every summer morning, and so did the singer who lived in the house opposite him.

The postman brought J. and D. Williams catalogues and would only give the parcel to the addressee and to no one else. He had squint eyes. But Murdo expected no letters. Nor did his mother.

Murdo had no theatre, no music, and hardly any books. He would buy milk from a loud stout deaf woman who shouted so that she could be heard all over the village. She had many sons who would hardly leave the house. They were odd people: but perhaps Murdo himself was odd. Who knows?

The war raged on. And Murdo listened to a wireless which was kept in a thatched house with a white cloth over it. (At this point Murdo would like to tell you of the rationale of thatched houses but in truth he is fatigued by this analysis of his youth and will not do so. Suffice it to say that the curvature of such a house is because of the high winds. Murdo however is not sentimental about the thatched house in which behind curtains in beds old women slept till they died. Murdo in fact thinks that microwaves and washing machines and tiles are a great improvement on the smoky benches of thatched houses.)

Suddenly the war came to a stop.

And Britain won. So after a while there might be sugar and sweets and oranges and jam instead of spam and whalemeat.

Thus Murdo like everyone else rejoiced. The young men ceased to be drowned though the young and old died of TB for there was no cure. In the sanatorium they spat and whitened and were like candles fading away, and they had hectic red spots on their cheeks, and Murdo was frightened of visiting his consumptive friends who were put out into the cold winds to be cured from the heat that was destroying them.

But Murdo himself, though thin, remained healthy enough and his bronchitis ceased, though his puzzlement at the universe increased. And he hid from it inside crosswords and geometry and mathematics.

He wanted to leave. Oh yes, he wanted to leave the sighs and the deaths and the sorrows and the ... and the ... and the ...

Could one blame Murdo? Only one in Murdo's place could blame Murdo. For Murdo was not suited to the island. He was not practical enough. And the wooden tables he had tried to carve looked like bedposts. So Murdo said Ave atque vale and Mrs Macleod said Good riddance. Who does he think he is with his Latin? Back of my hand to him and back of my neck also. Thus Mrs Macleod.

about the **author**

Iain Crichton Smith

Iain Crichton Smith was born on 1 January 1928 in Glasgow, and died in 1998. His parents were both from the Highlands, and in 1930 the family (there were three boys) moved to the island of Lewis. Shortly after the move Smith's father died. His widow brought up the boys in the small Lewis village of Bayble (home also to the Gaelic poet Derick Thomson). The family was poor – Smith reveals much of his own, his mother's and his brothers' difficulties (and their moments of delight) in his book of short stories about a Lewis boyhood in *On the Island* (1979). He went from his local school to the famous Nicholson Institute in Stornoway, and thence to Aberdeen University where he graduated in English Literature in 1949. In 1950–52 (after qualifying as a teacher) he had to undertake National Service, which he hated (the title story of the collection *Survival Wit' Error* (1970) reveals his anger at National authoritarianism and bullying barrack con family had moved to Dumbarton in 19

36

them and taught at Clydebank Academy till 1955, when he and his mother moved to Oban, where Iain taught English at the High School till 1977, when he decided to become a full-time writer. He married Donalda Logan in the same year; they moved to the village of Taynuilt, near Oban, where his widow continues to live. Smith was awarded the OBE in 1980, as well as receiving honorary doctorates from the universities of Glasgow, Dundee, and Aberdeen.

titles **by**

Iain Crichton Smith

Selected works

The Long River (1955); Burn is Aran (1960); Thistles and Roses (1961); Deer on the High Hills (1962); An Dubh is an Gorm (1963); Biobuill is Sansan Reice (1965); The Law and the Grace (1965); Modern Gaelic Verse (1966); The Golden Lyric: an Essay on the Poetry of Hugh MacDiarmid (1967); At Helensburgh (1968); Consider the Lilies (1968); Ben Dorain by Duncan Ban MacIntyre (1969); From Bourgeois Land (1969); The Last Summer (1969); Iain am Measg Nan Reultan (1970); Maighstirean is Ministearan (1970); Selected Poems (1970); Survival Without Error (1970); My Last Duchess (1971); Poems to Eimhir translated from Sorley MacLean (1971); Love Poems and Elegies (1972); An-t-Adhar Ameireaganach (1973); The Black and the Red (1970); Rabhdan is Rudan (1973); Eader Fealla-dha is Glaschu (1974); Goodbye Mr Dixon (1974); Hami Autumn (1974); The Notebooks of Robinson Crusoe (1975); The Permanent Island (1975); An t-Aonaran (1976); The Hermit and

Other Stories (1977); *An End to Autumn* (1978); *River, River* (1978); *On the Island* (1979); *Murdo* (1981); *A Field Full of Folk* (1982); *Selected Poems 1955–1982* (1982); *The Search* (1982); *Mr Trill in Hades* (1984); *The Exiles* (1984); *Selected Poems* (1985); *The Tenement* (1985); *Towards the Human: Selected Essays* (1986); ed., with C. King: *Twelve More Modern Scottish Poets* (1986); *A Life* (1986); *Burn is Aran* (1987); *An t-Eilean agus an Caan* (1987); *In the Middle of the Wood* (1987); ed., *Moments in Glasshouses* (1987); *A'Bheinn Oir* (1989); *Na Speuclairean Dubha* (1989); *The Dream* (1989); *Selected Poems* (1990); *Turas tro Shaoghal Falamh* (1991); *Na Guathan* (1991); *An Honourable Death* (1992); *Collected Poems* (1992) *An Dannsa mu Dheireadh* (1992).

discussion **points**

1. What constitutes 'normal' social behaviour?
   As we follow Murdo's antics, we often begin to recognise that his apparent irrationality and abnormal behaviour stems in fact from quite sane objections to aspects of modern society all too often accepted as normal. Murdo can thus be seen as questioning a huge range of such aspects, from the role of television in our lives to what is considered polite in community interchange. What are the major social issues challenged – including specifically local West Highland and small community issues, such as education, religion, welfare, transport, and cultural activities and values – all of which, from his early schooldays to his final 'autobiography', Murdo at some point – and in his own inimitable style – takes on?

2. Has Smith identified an unusually effective way of dealing with often painful and tragic issues? Or do we find Murdo too often selfish and simply banal for this to work consistently through the book?

3. How does the book hold together in its portrayal of a totally unpredictable man? The book appeared in three separate periods – so it might be interesting to assess whether the character of Murdo actually changes between the first story, with its background desperation, and the very different format of both the sixty-odd reflections and anecdotes which follow and the much more sober, yet still eccentric 'autobiography' of Smith/Murdo of the final part. Is there a unifying theme or idea? Or should we simply accept that since Murdo himself represents a fragmented mind in a broken world, so too does his book?

4. What is the relationship between Murdo and his author?
   Many of Smith's books handle personal issues through fiction; but this one teases the reader with its final admission that Smith is Murdo. Looking back over the volume, can this admission really stand up, given the varying personalities Murdo has exhibited? Or should we simply accept that something of the author's life will always appear to a greater or lesser extent in his fictions?

press **quotes**

'... there were places when I laughed until I cried. Murdo's utterances are a sardonic sideswipe at the world ...' – *The Times*

'... a delightful Don Quixote in a kilt, tilting at the windmills of the twentieth century... Murdo is a wonderful creation, a hoot and a half.'
– *Herald*

'He was a prolific, in English and Gaelic, and produced novels, short stories, essays, radio plays and stage plays as well as many volumes of poetry... his most popular work has always been the series of short stories about Murdo. Murdo is mad, but harmless. He shatters the complacent surface of life wherever he goes. He casts some doubts on the supremacy of reason. Like MacGonagall, he is perfectly serious, and that is what makes him so funny.'
– Edwin Morgan, *ScotLit*

'There is a fair measure of pain in his text, particularly when he is writing about his widowed mother – a relationship explored in some of his most powerful poems. But there is also much amusement and sly wit in the progress of the dreamy, skinny boy from Lewis into the adult world of university, National Service, teaching, and literary achievement.'

– Lesley Duncan, *Herald*

similar reads

Poetry

Readers of poetry will find Smith's ambivalent response to the harshness and beauty of his island background in collections like *Thistles and Roses* (1961) and *The Law and The Grace* (1965).

Fiction

In addition to *Consider the Lilies* (Canongate Books Ltd; ISBN: 0862411432) and *In The Middle of the Wood* (Gollancz; ISBN: 0575039671), there are deeply personal novels like *A Field Full of Folk* (1982, Gollancz; ISBN: 0575031107)(telling of a minister who loses his faith but recovers something arguably more important and human) and *The Search* (1982), which took Smith and his lifelong quest for meaning of Gaeldom, to Australia, and yet still on.

Short Stories

In short stories, the outstanding volume is *The Black and the Red* (1970, Gollancz; ISBN: 0575017058), with his recurrent dualism of vision, of darkness and colour. A selection of short stories appeared in *Listen to the Voice*

(Canongate Classics; ISBN: 0862414342) while a mixture of autobiography and essay can be found in his *Towards the Human* (1986, Saltire Publications; ISBN: 0863340598).

competition

Your chance to win ten contemporary works of fiction signed by their authors.

The *Read Around Books* series was developed by Scottish Book Trust to encourage readers to widen their reading interests and discover writers they had never tried before. Has it been a success? We want to hear from you. Tell us if you have enjoyed this little series or not and if you did, do you have any suggestions for authors who should be included in the series in the future.

Writer to us now with the following information:

Name and address
Email address
Are you a member of a readers' group?
Name of reader's group

Send us the information above and we will enter you into our prize draw to be drawn on 22 August 2003.

Send to:
RAB Draw
Scottish Book Trust
137 Dundee Street
Edinburgh EH11 1BG

scottish **book trust**

What is Scottish Book Trust?

Scottish Book Trust exists to serve readers and writers in Scotland. We work to ensure that everyone has access to good books, and to related resources and opportunities.

We do this in a number of ways:

- By operating the Writers in Scotland Scheme, which funds over 1,400 visits a year by Scottish writers to a variety of institutions and groups
- By supporting Scottish writing through a programme of professional training opportunities for writers
- By publishing a wide variety of resources and leaflets to support readership
- By promoting initiatives such as National Poetry Day and World Book Day
- And through our Book Information Service, providing free advice and support to readers and writers, and the general public.

For more information please visit
www.scottishbooktrust.com

titles **in the series**

Available in the Read Around Books series

Iain Crichton Smith's *Murdo: The Life and Works,*
    by Douglas Gifford

Meaghan Delahunt's *In The Blue House,*
    by Gavin Wallace

Michel Faber's *Under the Skin,* by Mary Firth

Jonathan Falla's *Blue Poppies,* by Rosemary Goring

Janice Galloway's *Clara,* by David Robinson

Andrew Greig's *That Summer,* by Alan Taylor

Anne MacLeod's *The Dark Ship,* by Lindsey Fraser

Maggie O'Farrell's *After You'd Gone,* by Rosemary Goring

Suhayl Saadi's *The Burning Mirror,*
    by Catherine McInerney

Ali Smith's *Hotel World,* by Kathryn Ross

Muriel Spark's *The Comforters,* by Alan Taylor

Alexander Trocchi's *Young Adam,* by Gillian Mackay